SING-ALONG
Car Songbook

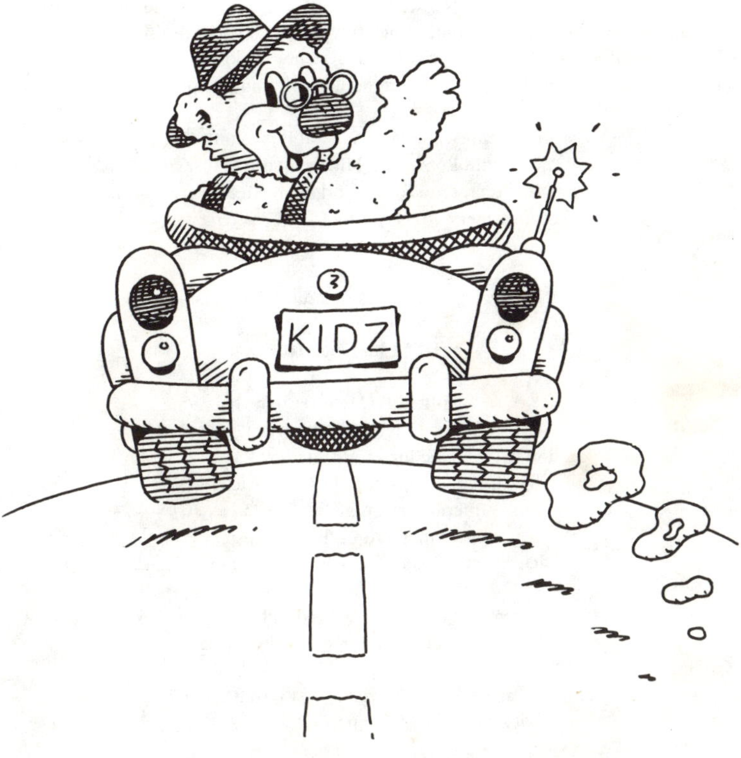

RUNNING PRESS • PHILADELPHIA

Copyright © 1992 by Running Press.
All rights reserved under the Pan-American and
International Copyright Conventions.

This book may not be reproduced in whole or in part in any form or by any
means, electronic or mechanical, including photocopying, recording, or by any
information storage and retrieval system now known or hereafter
invented, without written permission from the publisher.

Canadian representatives: General Publishing Co., Ltd.,
30 Lesmill Road, Don Mills, Ontario M3B 2T6.
International representatives: Worldwide Media Services, Inc.,
30 Montgomery Street, Jersey City, New Jersey 07302.

9 8 7 6 5 4 3 2 1
Digit on the right indicates the number of this printing

ISBN 1-56138-177-2 (package)

Edited by Melissa Stein
Cover design by Toby Schmidt
Station KIDZ Radio logo illustrated by Randy Hamblin
Cover illustrations by Mary Thelen
Interior design by Lili Schwartz
Interior illustrations by Len Epstein
Uncle Bumpy Roads™ illustrations by Fred Shrier
Typography: ITC Berkeley Oldstyle by
COMMCOR Communications Corporation, Philadelphia, Pennsylvania
Printed and bound in the United States

This package may be ordered by mail from the publisher.
Please add $2.50 for postage and handling.
Buy try your bookstore first!
Running Press Book Publishers
125 South Twenty-second Street
Philadelphia, Pennsylvania 19103

Contents

Old King Cole 7
    Traditional nursery rhyme

Gee, But I Want to Go Home 11
    Traditional American army song

Noble Duke of York 14
    Traditional English tune

A-Hunting We Will Go 16
    Traditional English song

Buffalo Gals 17
    Lyrics by Cool White

The Flying Trapeze 20
    Lyrics by George Leybourne

Shoo Fly 25
    Traditional Civil War song

A-Tisket A-Tasket 27
    Traditional play-party song

The Blue-Tail Fly (Jimmy Crack Corn) 29
    Lyrics by Dan Emmett

My Hat It Has Three Corners 32
    Traditional

My Old Kentucky Home 33
    Lyrics by Stephen C. Foster

John Henry 36
    Traditional

Good Old Summer Time 39
    Lyrics by Ren Shields

There Was an Old Lady Who Swallowed a Fly 44
    Traditional English song

Sweet Betsy from Pike 47
    Traditional American wagon train song
Waltzing Matilda 51
    Lyrics by Andrew Barton Paterson
Little Brown Jug 55
    Lyrics by J.E. Winner
Looby Loo 57
    Traditional singing game
Punchinello 60
    Traditional American song
Daisy Bell 62
    Lyrics by Harry Dacre
Billy Boy 65
    Traditional nursery rhyme
Golden Slippers 68
    Lyrics by James A. Bland
The Riddle Song (I Gave My Love A Cherry) 72
    Traditional American song
If All the World Were Paper 74
    Traditional English country dance tune
There's A Hole in the Bucket 75
    Traditional Pennsylvania German song
What Did Delaware? 79
    Traditional
Go to Sleepy (All the Pretty Little Horses) 82
    Traditional
Home Sweet Home 83
    Traditional
Bye Baby Bunting 85
    Traditional
Short'nin' Bread 86
    Traditional Southern American song
Goodnight Ladies 89
    Traditional
The Animal Fair 91
    Traditional American minstrel song

There's A Hole in the Middle of the Sea 93
    Traditional

I Love Little Pussy 97
    Traditional nursery rhyme

John Brown's Body 98
    Lyrics by Charles S. Hall

Lucy Locket 101
    Traditional nursery rhyme

Ladybird 102
    Lyrics by Robert Schumann

Old Folks at Home (Swanee River) 105
    Stephen C. Foster

Patsy-Orey-Orey-Ay 108
    Traditional Irish song

Shanghai Chicken 112
    Traditional American song

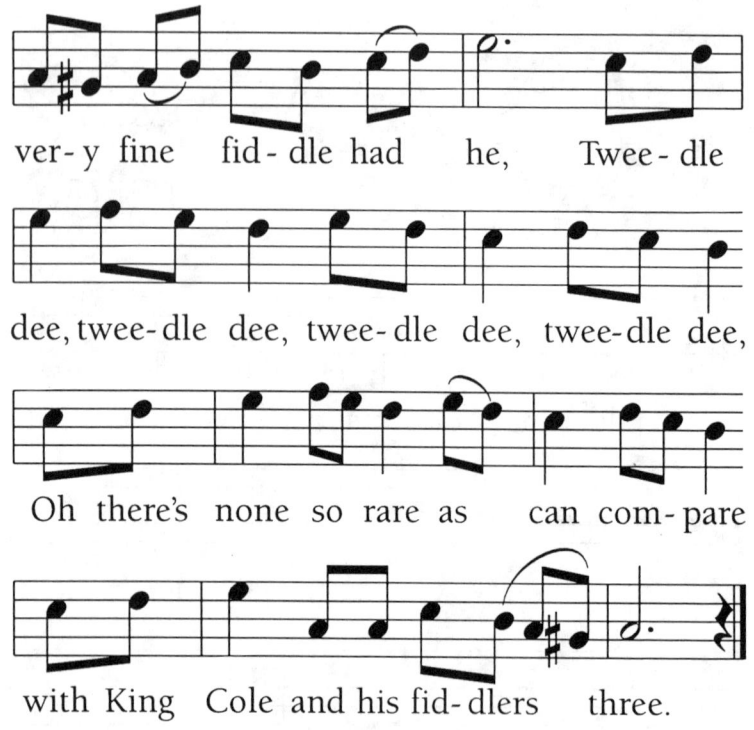

2

Old King Cole
Was a merry old soul,
And a merry old soul was he;
He called for his pipe,
And he called for his bowl,
And he called for his harpers three.
Ev'ry harper he had a fine harp,
And a very fine harp had he;
Twang-a-twang, twang-a-twang, twang-a-twang,
   twang-a-twang,
Tweedle dee, tweedle dee, tweedle dee,
   tweedle dee;
O there's none so rare
As can compare
With King Cole and his fiddlers three.

3

Old King Cole
Was a merry old soul,
And a merry old soul was he;
He called for his pipe,
And he called for his bowl,
And he called for his pipers three.
Ev'ry piper he had a fine pipe,
And a very fine pipe had he;
Tootle too, tootle too, tootle too, tootle too,

Twang-a-twang, twang-a-twang, twang-a-twang,
   twang-a-twang,
Tweedle dee, tweedle dee, tweedle dee,
   tweedle dee;
O there's none so rare
As can compare
With King Cole and his fiddlers three.

2

The biscuits that they give you
They say are mighty fine;
One rolled off a table
And it killed a pal of mine.

Chorus

3

The chickens that they give you
They say are mighty fine;
One rolled off a table
And it started marking time.

Chorus

4

The details that they give us
They say are mighty fine
The garbage that we pick up
They feed us all the time.

Chorus

5

The clothing that they give you
They say are mighty fine,
But me and my buddy
Can both fit into mine.

Chorus

6

The women in the service club
They say are mighty fine,
But most are over ninety
And the rest are under nine.

Chorus

The Noble Duke of York

Oh, the no-ble Duke of York, he had ten thou-sand men; he marched them up to the top of the hill and he marched them down a-gain.

2

Now when they were up, they were up;
And when they were down, they were down;
And when they were only halfway up,
They were neither up nor down.

come out to-night, come out to-night?

Buf-fa-lo Gals, won't you come out to-night

and dance by the light of the moon.

2

I asked her would she have some talk,
Have some talk, have talk,
I asked her would she have some talk
As she stood close to me.

Chorus

3

I asked her would she like to dance
Like to dance, like to dance,
I asked her would she like to dance
As she stood close to me.

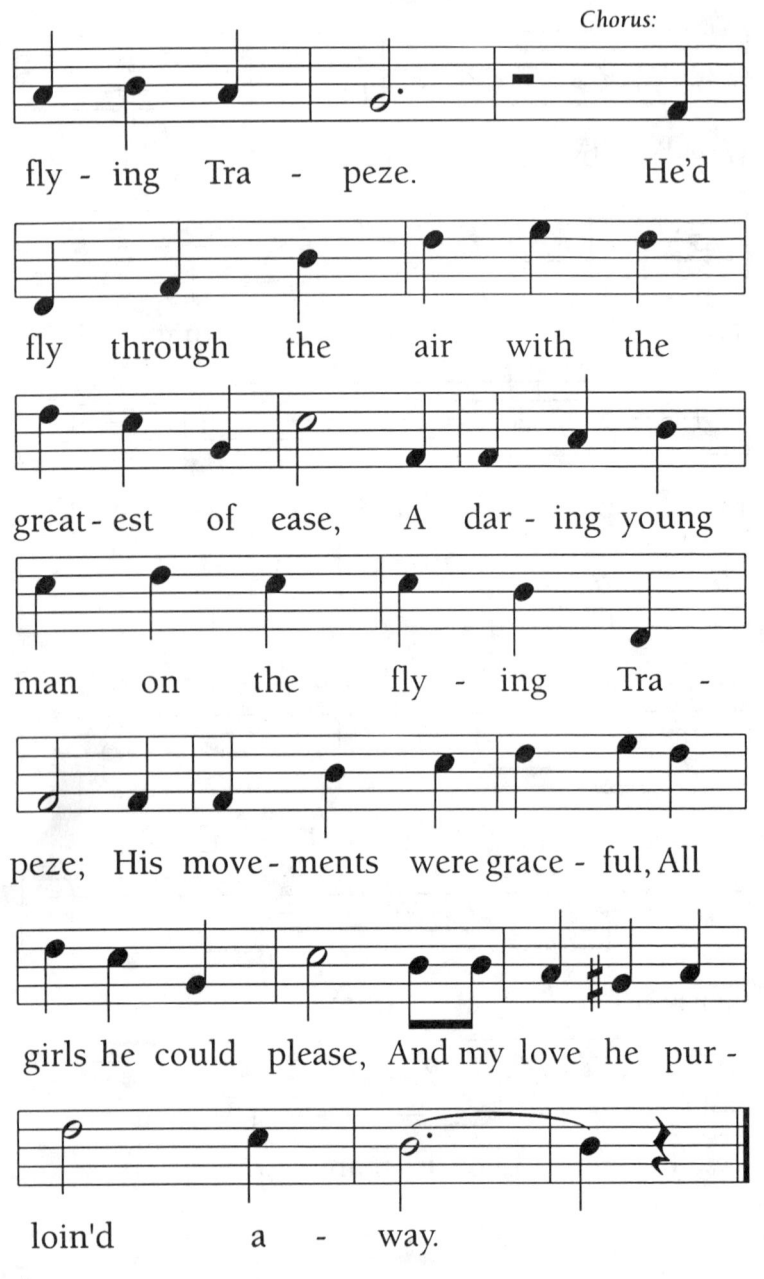

2

This young man by name was Signor Bonaslang—
Tall, big, and handsome; as well made as Chang.
Where'er he appeared, the hall loudly rang
With ovation from all people there.
He'd smile from the bar on the people below,
And one night he smiled on my love.
She winked back at him and she shouted "Bravo!"
As he hung by his nose up above.

Chorus

3

One night I, as usual, went to her home,
Found there her father and mother alone.
I asked for my love, and soon they made known,
To my horror, that she'd run away.
She'd packed up her box and eloped in the night
With him, with the greatest of ease—
From two stories high, he had lowered her down
To the ground on his flying trapeze.

Chorus for last verse:
She floats through the air
With the greatest of ease.
You'd think her a man on the flying trapeze.
She does all the work
While he takes his ease
And that's what became of my love.

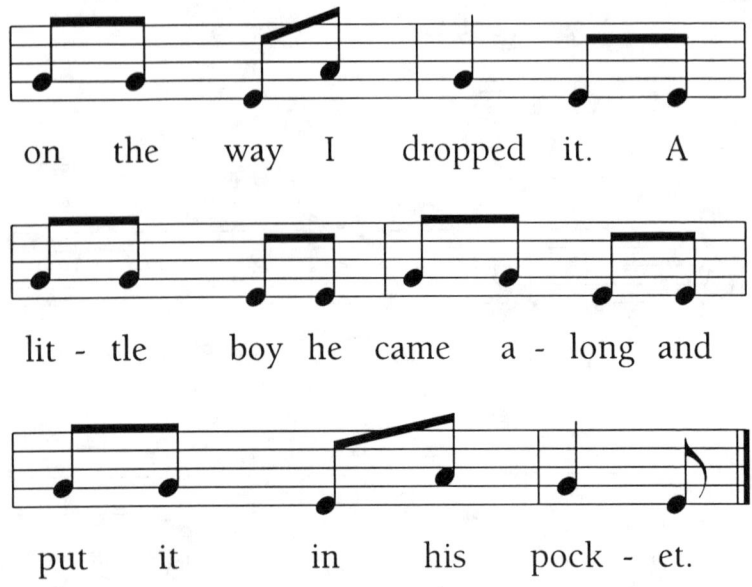

I don't care, Jim-my crack corn and

I don't care, Jim-my crack corn and

I don't care, my mas-ter's gone a - way.

2

When he'd ride in the afternoon,
I'd follow with a hickory broom;
The pony being rather shy,
Was bitten by a blue-tail fly.

Chorus

3

Once when he rode around the farm,
The flies about him thick did swarm,
The pony which was rather shy
Was bitten by the blue-tail fly.

Chorus

4

The pony run, he jump, he pitch,
He threw my Master in a ditch;
He died and the jury wondered why
The verdict was the blue-tail fly.

Chorus

5

They laid him under a 'simmon tree,
His epitaph is there to see;
"Beneath this stone I'm forced to lie,
A victim of the blue-tail fly."

Chorus

sing one song for the old Ken-tuck-y Home,

For the old Ken-tuck-y Home, far a-way.

could - n't keep it from the boy.

He was born a ham - mer hit - tin' boy.

2

When John Henry, speaking to the foreman,
Said "A man should prove himself a man,
And before I'd let your steam drill beat me
    down,
I'll die with the hammer in my hand, O Lord!
Die with the hammer in my hand."

3

When John Henry had a little offspring,
And he took him gently on his knee,
And he hugged him and he kissed him, while
    he said:
"My son, always do the best you can,
Try to do the best you can, like me."

4

When John Henry took a heavy hammer,
And, beside the steam drill he did stand,
He was faster than the drill, but Oh! alas,
He died with the hammer in his hand, O Lord!
Died with the hammer in his hand.

5

So they took John Henry to the graveyard,
And they laid him down into the sand,
And when any locomotive passed the grave,
'Tis said the engineer would look and say:
"There lies a steel-drivin' man."

In the Good Old Summer Time

There's a time in each year that we al-ways hold dear, Good old sum-mer time; With the birds and the trees-es and sweet scent-ed breez-es;

continued next page

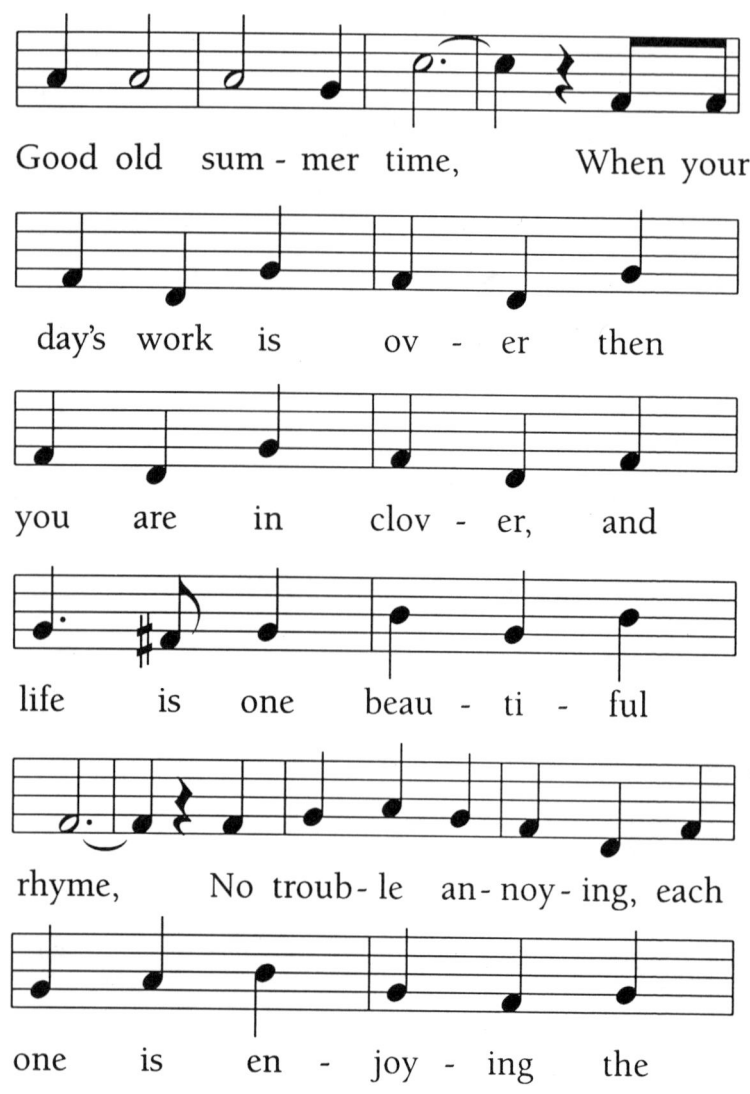

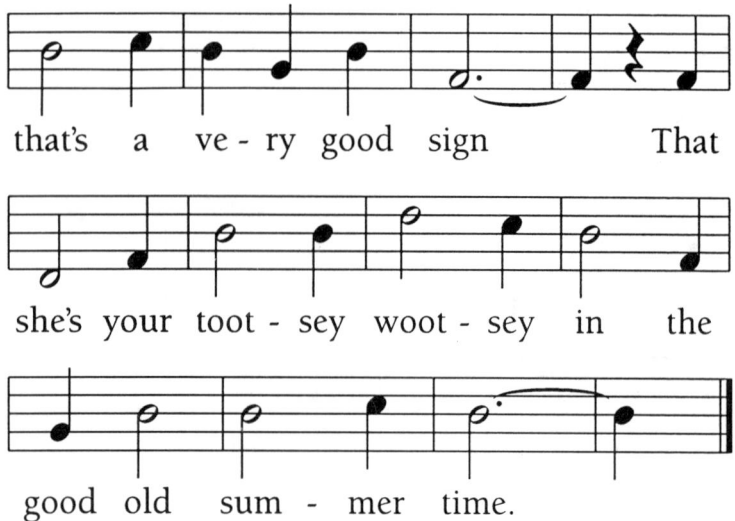

2

To swim in the pool you'd play "hooky" from school,
Good old summer time,
You'd play "ring a rosie" with Jim, Kate and Josie,
Good old summer time,
Those days full of pleasure we now fondly treasure,
When we never thought it a crime
To go stealing cherries, with face brown as berries,
Good old summer time.

Chorus

3

There was an old lady who swallowed a bird,
Now, ain't it absurd to swallow a bird;
She swallowed the bird to catch the spider,
She swallowed the spider to catch the fly . . .

4

There was an old lady who swallowed a cat,
Now fancy that, to swallow a cat . . .

5

There was an old lady who swallowed a dog,
Oh, what a hog to swallow a dog . . .

6

There was an old lady who swallowed a cow,
I don't know how she swallowed a cow . . .

7

There was an old lady who swallowed a horse,
SHE DIED, OF COURSE!

2

One evening quite early, they camped by a stream.
To reach California, oh that was their dream.
The Shanghai was "et" but the cattle just died,
The last strip of bacon that morning was fried.

Chorus

3

Came the Injuns from nowhere, a wild yelling horde.
And Betsy was skeered as she prayed to the Lord.
Behind their big wagon the couple did crawl,
And they fought off the Injuns with musket and ball.

Chorus

4

Then they swam the wide rivers and crossed the tall peaks,
And lived on wild berries and water for weeks.
Starvation and hard work and sun-stroke as well,
But they reached California in spite of all hell.

Chorus

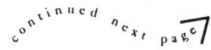

5

They were six months in Frisco, when Ike met
    a girl,
A sweet looking dancer who gave him a twirl.
He spoke of poor Betsy as "just an old horse,"
What was Betsy to do? She gave Ike his divorce.

Chorus

6

She left Frisco and went back to Pike so they
    say,
And Ike lost his dancer and soon passed away.
If this tale is touching, go cry if you like
Mighty fine kind of woman! Sweet Betsy from
    Pike.

Chorus

2

Down came a jumbuck to drink beside the billabong.
Up jumped the swagman and seized him with glee,
And he sang as he tucked that jumbuck in his tucker bag,
"You'll come a-waltzing Matilda with me.
Waltzing Matilda, waltzing Matilda,
You'll come a-waltzing Matilda with me.
And he sang as he tucked that jumbuck in his tucker bag,
"You'll come a-waltzing Matilda with me."

3

Down came the stock man, riding on his thoroughbred;
Down came the troopers, one, two, three:
"Where's the jolly jumbuck you've got in your tucker bag?
You'll come a-waltzing Matilda with me,"
Waltzing Matilda, waltzing Matilda,
You'll come a-waltzing Matilda with me.
"Where's the jolly jumbuck you've got in your tucker bag?
You'll come a-waltzing Matilda with me."

continued next page

4

Up jumped the swagman and plunged into the billabong.

"You'll never catch me alive!" cried he.

And his ghost may be heard as you ride beside the billabong:

"You'll come a-waltzing Matilda with me."

Waltzing Matilda, waltzing Matilda,

You'll come a-waltzing Matilda with me.

And his ghost may be heard as you ride beside the billabong:

"You'll come a-waltzing Matilda with me."

Little Brown Jug

My wife and I live

all a-lone, In a lit-tle log hut we

call our own. She loves gin and

I love rum, Be-tween us we have

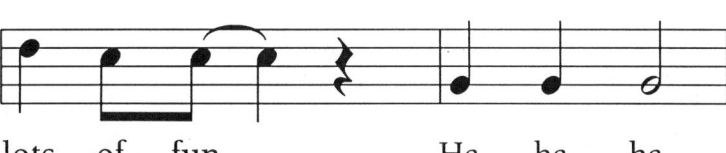

lots of fun. Ha ha ha,

continued next page

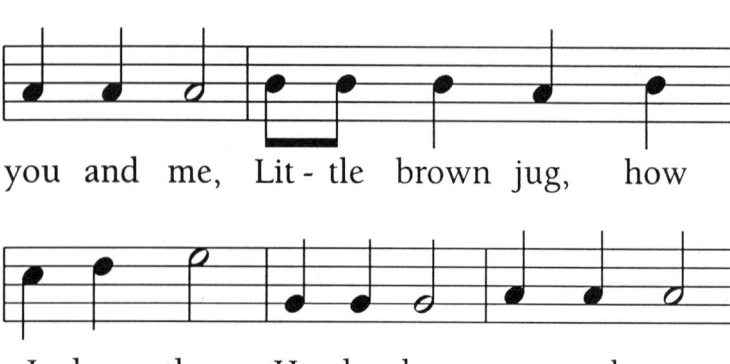

2

I put my left hand in,
I put my left hand out,
I give my left hand a shake, shake, shake,
And turn myself about.

*Repeat for "my right foot,"
"my left foot," and
"my whole self."*

2

Look who is there,
Punchinello, funny fellow?
Look who is there,
Punchinello, funny boy?

3

What can you do,
Punchinello, funny fellow?
What can you do,
Punchinello, funny boy?

4

We can do it too,
Punchinello, funny fellow
We can do it too,
Punchinello, funny boy.

5

You choose one of us,
Punchinello, funny fellow,
You choose one of us,
Punchinello, funny boy.

Daisy Bell

There is a flow-er with-in my heart, Dai-sy, Dai-sy! Plant-ed one day by a glanc-ing dart, Plan-ted by Dai-sy Bell! Wheth-er she loves me or

won't be a styl - ish marr - iage; I can't af - ford a carr - iage. But you'll look sweet on the seat of a bi - cy - cle built for two!

2

Did she bid you to come in,
Billy Boy, Billy Boy?
Did she bid you to come in,
Charming Billy?
Yes, she bade me to come in,
There's a dimple in her chin.
She's a young thing
And cannot leave her mother.

3

Did she set for you a chair?
Billy Boy, Billy Boy?
Did she set for you a chair,
Charming Billy?
Yes, she set for me a chair,
She has ringlets in her hair,
She's a young thing
And cannot leave her mother.

4

Can she make a cherry pie,
Billy Boy, Billy Boy?
Can she make a cherry pie,
Charming Billy?

She can make a cherry pie,
Quick as a cat can wink her eye,
She's a young thing
And cannot leave her mother.

5

Can she sing a pretty song,
Billy Boy, Billy Boy?
Can she sing a pretty song,
Charming Billy?
She can sing a pretty song,
But she often sings it wrong,
She's a young thing
And cannot leave her mother.

6

How old is she,
Billy Boy, Billy Boy?
How old is she,
Charming Billy?
Three times six and four times seven,
Twenty-eight and eleven!
She's a young thing
And cannot leave her mother.

2

There's the long white robe that I bought last June,
That I must go and change because it fits too soon,
And the old grey horse that I always drive,
I will hitch up to the chariot in the morn.

Chorus

3

And my banjo still is hanging on the wall,
For it hasn't had a tune-up since away last fall.
But the folks all say we'll have a fine old time,
When we ride up in the chariot in the morn.

Chorus

4

So it's goodbye, children, I will have to go
Where the rain can't fall and the wind won't blow,
And your ulster coats you never there will need
When we ride up in the chariot in the morn.

Chorus

5

Now, your golden slippers must be shiny clean,
And your gloves the very whitest that were ever
    seen,
And be sure you're ready when it's time to go,
When we ride up in the chariot in the morn.

Chorus

2

How can there be a cherry that has no stone?
How can there be a chicken that has no bone?
How can there be a ring that has no end?
How can there be a baby that's no cryin'?

3

A cherry when it's blooming it has no stone,
A chicken when it's pipping it has no bone,
A ring when it's rolling it has no end,
A baby when it's sleeping there's no cryin'.

There's a Hole in the Bucket

There's a hole in the buck-et, dear Li - za, dear Li- za, There's a hole in the

buck - et, dear Li - za, There's a hole. Well,

fix it, dear Hen- ry, dear

2

With what shall I fix it, dear Liza, dear Liza,
With what shall I fix it, dear Liza, with what?
With a straw, dear Henry, dear Henry, dear Henry,
With a straw, dear Henry, dear Henry, with a straw.

3

But the straw is too long, dear Liza, dear Liza,
But the straw is too long, dear Liza, too long.
Then cut it, dear Henry, dear Henry, dear Henry,
Then cut it, dear Henry, dear Henry, then cut it.

4

Well, how shall I cut it, dear Liza, dear Liza,
Well, how shall I cut it, dear Liza, well, how?
With a knife, dear Henry, dear Henry, dear Henry,
With a knife, dear Henry, dear Henry, with a knife.

5

But the knife is too dull, dear Liza, dear Liza,
But the knife is too dull, dear Liza, too dull.
Then sharpen it, dear Henry, dear Henry, dear Henry,
Then sharpen it, dear Henry, dear Henry, then sharpen it.

6

With what shall I sharpen it, dear Liza, dear Liza,
With what shall I sharpen it, dear Liza, with what?
With a whetstone, dear Henry, dear Henry, dear Henry,
With a whetstone, dear Henry, dear Henry, with a whetstone.

7

But the whetstone's too dry, dear Liza, dear Liza,
But the whetstone's too dry, dear Liza, too dry.
Then wet it, dear Henry, dear Henry, dear Henry,
Then wet it, dear Henry, dear Henry, then wet it.

8

With what shall I wet it, dear Liza, dear Liza,
With what shall I wet it, dear Liza, with what?
With water, dear Henry, dear Henry, dear Henry,
With water, dear Henry, dear Henry, with water.

What did Delaware?

Oh what did Del-a-ware, boys, Oh

what did Del-a-ware? Oh, what did Del-a-

ware, boys, Oh what did Del-a-ware? She

wore her new Jer-sey, boys, She wore her

new Jer - sey.   I   tell you now as a

per - son - al friend, She wore her new Jer - sey.

2

Oh what did I-o-way, boys,
Oh what did I-o-way?
Oh, what did I-o-way, boys,
Oh what did I-o-way,
She weighed a Wash-ing-ton, boys,
She weighed a Wash-ing-ton.
I tell you now as a personal friend,
She weighed a Wash-ing-ton.

3

Oh what did Ten-nes-see, boys,
Oh what did Ten-nes-see?
Oh, what did Ten-nes-see, boys
Oh what did Ten-nes-see,
She saw what Ar-kan-sas, boys,
She saw what Ar-kan-sas.
I tell you now as a personal friend,
She saw what Ar-kan-sas.

Go to Sleepy (All the Pretty Little Horses)

Hush you bye, Don't you cry,

Go to sleep-y, lit-tle ba - by;

When you wake, You shall have cake, And

drive those pret-ty lit-tle hor-ses.

there, Which, seek through the world, is ne-ver met else-where.

Home, home, sweet, sweet home!

There's no place like home there's no place like home.

Short'nin' Bread

Three lit-tle ba-bies ly-in' in bed,

Two were sick and the oth-er 'most dead.

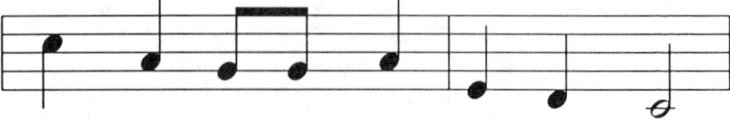
Sent for the doc-tor and the doc-tor said,

"Give those ba-bies some short-'nin' bread."

Chorus:

Mam-my's lit-tle ba-by loves short-'nin',

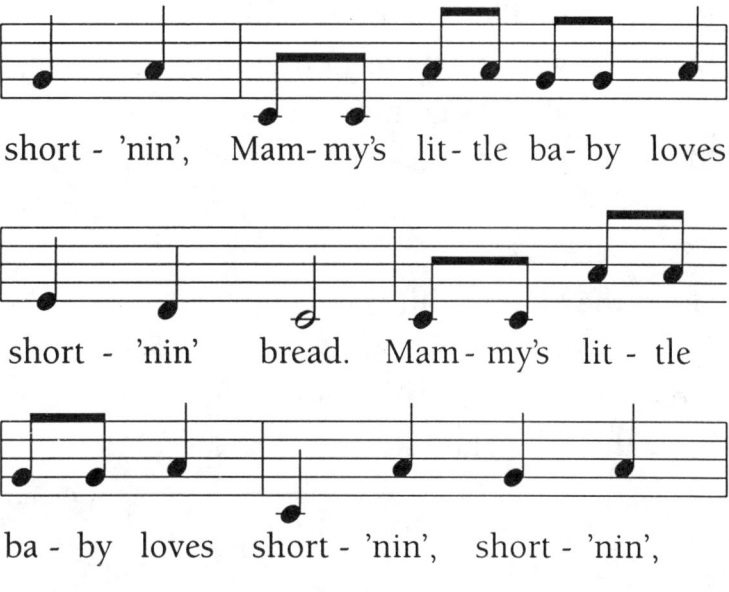

2

Put on the skillet, put on the lid,
Mammy's goin' to make a little short'nin' bread,
That isn't all she's goin' to do,
Mammy's goin' to make a little coffee, too.

Chorus

3

Go in the kitchen, lift up the lid,
Fill my pockets with short'nin' bread;
Stole the skillet, stole the lid,
Stole the gal makin' short'nin' bread.

Chorus

2

Farewell, ladies!
Farewell, ladies!
Farewell, ladies!
We're going to leave you now.

Chorus

3

Sweet dreams, ladies!
Sweet dreams, ladies!
Sweet dreams, ladies!
We're going to leave you now.

Chorus

The Animal Fair

I went to The An-i-mal Fair, The

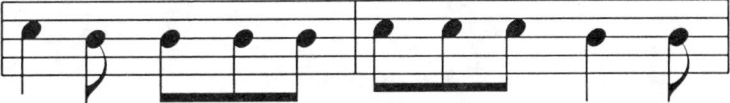

birds and the beasts were there, The

big ba-boon, by the light of the moon, was

comb-ing his au-burn hair; You

ought to have seen the monk, He

continued next page

jumped on the el-e-phant's trunk; The

el-e-phant sneezed and fell on his knees, And

what be-came of the monk?

There's a Hole in the Middle of the Sea

There's a hole in the mid-dle of the

sea, There's a hole in the mid-dle of the

sea, There's a hole, there's a hole,

There's a hole in the mid-dle of the sea.

continued next page

2

There's a log in the hole in the middle of the sea.
There's a log in the hole in the middle of the sea.
There's a log, there's a log,
There's a log in the hole in the middle of the sea.

3

There's a bump on the log in the hole in the middle of the sea.
There's a bump on the log in the hole in the middle of the sea.
There's a bump, there's a bump,
There's a bump on the log in the hole in the middle of the sea.

4

There's a frog on the bump on the log in the hole in the middle of the sea.
There's a frog on the bump on the log in the hole in the middle of the sea.
There's a frog, there's a frog,
There's a frog on the bump on the log in the hole in the middle of the sea.

5

There's a fly on the frog on the bump on the log
 in the hole in the middle of the sea.
There's a fly on the frog on the bump on the log
 in the hole in the middle of the sea.
There's a fly, there's a fly,
There's a fly on the frog on the bump on the log
 in the hole in the middle of the sea.

6

There's a wing on the fly on the frog on the
 bump on the log in the hole in the middle
 of the sea.
There's a wing on the fly on the frog on the
 bump on the log in the hole in the middle
 of the sea.
There's a wing, there's a wing,
There's a wing on the fly on the frog on the
 bump on the log in the hole in the middle
 of the sea.

7

There's a flea on the wing on the fly on the frog
 on the bump on the log in the hole in the
 middle of the sea.
There's a flea on the wing on the fly on the frog
 on the bump on the log in the hole in the
 middle of the sea.
There's a flea, there's a flea,
There's a flea on the wing on the fly on the frog
 on the bump on the log in the hole in the
 middle of the sea.

2

Stars in Heaven are all looking kindly down,
Stars in Heaven are all looking kindly down,
Stars in Heaven are all looking kindly down,
His soul goes marching on!

Chorus

3

John Brown's knapsack is strapped upon his back,
John Brown's knapsack is strapped upon his back,
John Brown's knapsack is strapped upon his back,
His soul goes marching on!

Chorus

4

He's gone to be a soldier in the army of the Lord,
He's gone to be a soldier in the army of the Lord,
He's gone to be a soldier in the army of the Lord,
His soul goes marching on!

Chorus

Ladybird

Come, La-dy-bird, and seat your-self up-on my hand, up-on my hand; Be sure I will not harm you, No, I'll not harm you! I will not harm you, pret-ty dear,

Show your pret-ty wings and nev-er fear,

Ti - ny wings so gay and pret- ty.

2

Go, Ladybird, fly home, fly home,
'Tis all on fire, your children cry
So sorely, oh, so sorely,
Cry, cry so sorely!
The cunning spider spins them in,
Ladybird, make haste; fly in, fly in,
To your children crying sorely.

3

Fly, Ladybird, now fly away
Across the hedge, across the hedge,
The neighbors will not harm you,
No, they'll not harm you!
They will not harm you, pretty dear,
Show your tiny wings and never fear,
Give them all a cheery greeting.

2

All around the little farm I wandered when I
  was young,
There many happy days I've squandered, there
  many songs I've sung.
When I was playing with my brother, happy
  was I,
Oh, take me to my kind old mother, there let
  me live and die.

3

One little hut among the bushes, one that I
  love,
Still sadly to my memory rushes, no matter
  where I rove.
When will I see the bees a-humming all around
  the comb?
When will I hear the banjo tumming, down in
  my good old home?

Pat - sy - Or - ey - Or - ey - Ay,

Pat - sy - Or - ey - Or - ey - Ay,

Work - ing on the rail - road.

2

In eighteen hundred and ninety-two,
Looking around for something to do,
Looking around for something to do,
Working on the railroad.

Chorus

3

In eighteen hundred and ninety-three,
The overseer accepted me,
The overseer accepted me,
Working on the railroad.

Chorus

4

In eighteen hundred and ninety-four,
Hands and feet were getting sore,
Hands and feet were getting sore,
Working on the railroad.

Chorus

5

In eighteen hundred and ninety-five,
Found myself more dead than alive,
Found myself more dead than alive,
Working on the railroad.

Chorus

6

In eighteen hundred and ninety-six,
Dropped a couple of dynamite sticks,
Dropped a couple of dynamite sticks,
Working on the railroad.

Chorus

7

In eighteen hundred and ninety-seven,
Took a flying trip to Heaven,
Took a flying trip to Heaven,
Working on the railroad.

Chorus

8

In eighteen hundred and ninety-eight,
I picked the lock on the Golden Gate,
I picked the lock on the Golden Gate,
Working on the railroad.

Chorus

9

In eighteen hundred and ninety-nine,
I got my harp and wings divine,
I got my harp and wings divine,
Working on the railroad.

Chorus

2

Gret big fish they call a whale;
Few days, few days;
Swallowed Jonah head and tail,
And I'm goin' home.

I have a home over yonder;
Few days, few days;
I have a home over yonder,
And I'm goin' home.